CONTENTS

	Introduction	5
1.	Gardens	7
2.	Churches	23
3.	Cliffs & Sands	31
4.	Transport	45
5.	Central Bournemouth & The Square	55
6.	Shops	71
7.	The Pier	77
8.	Events	87
9.	Hotels	103
10.	Boscombe	111
11.	The Russell-Cotes Family	119
	Acknowledgements	126

East Cliff Hall, 1907. The home of the Russell-Cotes Art Gallery and Museum.

To Peter & Val
August 2015
Hugh & Susan Rayner

BOURNEMOUTH

ALISON CRAWFORD

The Russell-Cotes Art Gallery and Museum was founded in 1907 when Sir Merton and Lady Russell-Cotes gave their home, East Cliff Hall, and its contents to the people of Bournemouth. Their collections were primarily formed in the last quarter of the nineteenth century from their extensive travels abroad, bringing home souvenirs of the countries they visited. The most significant was their trip to Japan in 1885 from which they brought back over one hundred crates. They also founded an Irving Museum within East Cliff Hall, dedicated to the great Victorian actor, Sir Henry Irving. This includes his personal items, props and mementos of his and his contemporaries such as Ellen Terry, Lewis Waller and Sarah Bernhardt.

Sir Merton's painting collection filled almost every inch of wall space, while ceramics, metalwork, natural history artefacts, ethnography, furniture and sculpture filled the rooms. The house itself, now a Grade II* listed building, was based on the Scottish Baronial and Italianate villa and designed by the architect John Frederick Fogerty in 1897. Its lavish interiors included copies of the Parthenon frieze and a Moorish alcove based on designs from the Alhambra in Granada. Rich in Tynecastle embossed wallpapers, stencils and stained glass, East Cliff Hall is as much of interest as the collections it houses.

The museum and the collection have grown since then, with four purpose-built art galleries and a modern extension for temporary exhibitions, a café and educational facilities. If you are interested in finding out more then write or telephone us at:

The Russell-Cotes Art Gallery & Museum
East Cliff
Bournemouth
Dorset BH1 3AA
Tel: 01202 451858
Fax: 01202 451851
email: r-c.enquiries@bournemouth.gov.uk

Or why not visit our web site at www.russell-cotes.bournemouth.gov.uk.

From the collection of the Russell-Cotes Art Gallery and Museum

First published 1998
This edition first published 2009

The History Press
The Mill, Brimscombe Port
Stroud, Gloucestershire, GL5 2QG
www.thehistorypress.co.uk

ISBN 978 0 7524 4943 2

Typesetting and origination by The History Press
Printed in Great Britain

INTRODUCTION

Compared with its older neighbours of Christchurch and Poole, Bournemouth does not have the ancient buildings or material evidence of an historic town. Prehistoric remains have been found in the area and small communities existed further inland, but the area surrounding the mouth of the Bourne stream was wild and desolate heathland, common land used for grazing and a convenient and deserted smuggling site. In 1805 much of the common land was enclosed and sold to seven freeholders. This cleared the way for individuals to do something with the site, although there were little immediate effects. Plantations of pine trees replaced much of the gorse and heath, roads were developed from previous rough tracks and an inn was established to provide facilities between Christchurch and Poole.

The site of Bournemouth had been seen as a possible place for an enemy to land for centuries. During the Napoleonic Wars, from the late eighteenth century, a Captain Lewis Tregonwell was the commander responsible for defence of the area. He revisited the site with his wife in 1810 and they decided to buy a portion of land and build a house here, an event which is generally seen as the foundation of Bournemouth.

The other landowners were also beginning to realise the potential of the area, especially with regard to the growing Victorian passion for the seaside. This had developed largely from the previous age's enthusiasm for spa towns. In the mid-eighteenth century it was proclaimed that sea water was just as good for you as spa water, and so the centres of fashion and excess gradually expanded from the inland spa towns to the coastal resorts.

Most of these resorts had previously existed in some form, usually as fishing villages. Bournemouth, although blessed with sandy beaches and a warm climate, almost had to start from scratch. This and its remote location from London meant it was slow to develop into a seaside resort, but it was this opportunity that transformed the site of Bournemouth so rapidly and successfully.

By the 1850s Bournemouth was beginning to take shape and it was obvious that some sort of independence was needed if the development was to continue in a beneficial manner. This need led to the Bournemouth Improvement Act of 1856 and a Board of Commissioners, who ensured that the interests of the town were foremost. They set about providing Bournemouth with the facilities and publicity it needed to become a popular resort. Its growth from this time can be measured to some extent by the increase in population. In 1851 the census recorded just 695 people in the Bournemouth district. Within twenty years this figure leapt to nearly 6,000 and ten years later, in 1881, to nearly 17,000.

During the nineteenth century the social tone of a resort was as important as its facilities. Brighton, largely owing to patronage from the Prince Regent, was seen as highly fashionable, if a little risqué. Margate, easily accessible by Londoners, was seen as a little low and common. Bournemouth had proclaimed its advantages as a health restorer from the start. This, and its inaccessibility to anyone other than those with time and money on their hands, led to the image of a centre for the wealthy sick and elderly.

This image has gradually altered with industrial and social progress. Developments in transportation combined with increased time off for workers meant that short holidays and eventually day trips to Bournemouth were possible. These factors have also led to an increase in permanent Bournemouth residents. The appeal of the seaside day trip or holiday has prevailed and present-day developments prove that the town is continuing its original efforts to attract visitors.

Much of the making of Bournemouth coincided with the development of photography. In some cases we are able to view photographic images of change from untouched land to development, which is impossible in towns where man had already altered the scene.

The photographs in this book have been selected only from the Russell-Cotes Art Gallery and Museum collection and as such are not a complete representation of all the stages in Bournemouth's developing history. However, it is hoped that the images show not only some of the remarkable changes that have occurred, but also something of the experiences of holidaymakers and residents over the passing decades.

CHAPTER ONE

GARDENS

The Victorian pleasure seeker would expect a fashionable town to have gardens. They were a public place for relaxation, entertainment, exercise and play. In Bournemouth gardens had the added function of providing a safe, level and sheltered place for invalids to stretch their limbs. We are fortunate that much of Bournemouth was planned at a time when gardens were so popular, as much prime land was dedicated to this use and has escaped development.

The first gardens in Bournemouth were the Westover Pleasure Gardens, set on the slope of the south side of Westover Road and facing the prestigious Westover Villas. They were laid out in 1848–9 and replaced rough fir and bramble plantation with laurel, ornamental shrubs and grassy glades. Access was provided through oak gates on to paths which linked the main areas of the town, two rustic bridges covered the Bourne Stream and the whole area was enclosed with rustic fencing. The gardens were maintained by a committee and residents paid a yearly charge for their use.

The valley at the bottom of Westover Gardens, where the familiar Lower Gardens are now, remained as rough, marshy grassland which could flood with a high tide and where horses and cattle were often put out to graze. It wasn't until 1869 that preparations were made to turn this area into an extension of the Westover Gardens. The land had to be drained and levelled – a difficult and lengthy process, but by 1873 the area was beginning to take shape.

On the other side of the bridge, or Square, similar work was being carried out to create the lengthy Upper Gardens. Mansions and large villas were built on both sides of the shallow valley, giving the occupants an enviable vista on to the pretty gardens.

Upper Gardens from Queen's Road, 1867. This view is a good illustration of how marshy and desolate the area was before draining and landscaping. The large house to the right of centre is Eastbury in Surrey Road.

Upper Gardens, 1870s. Again, the natural state of the area is evident. The imposing house in the background of this view is Hume Towers, a brick mansion set in 12 acres and built in 1870. For the first thirty years of its existence Hume Towers was mainly let by its owners to the likes of the Earl and Countess of Bradford and Lord and Lady Wimborne. In 1899 it became the home of Sir William Earnshaw Cooper, who died there in 1924. In 1926 Hume Towers opened as a luxurious convalescent home, specialising in providing treatment for those suffering nervous breakdowns. Now replaced by houses, it occupied the whole site in Branksome Wood Road between Leven Avenue and Benellen Avenue.

Upper Gardens and the Sanatorium, 1870s. Bournemouth was chosen as an ideal place for a sanatorium because it possessed the three main qualities beneficial to health: dryness, equability and mildness of temperature. The Sanatorium, for consumption and diseases of the chest, was opened in Bourne Avenue in 1855 for the reception of forty female sufferers. Ornamental shrubs have been planted, although there is still a 'new' look to the gardens.

Upper Gardens. The Sanatorium, The Glen and Richmond Hill Congregational church can be seen in Bourne Avenue. The Glen was a large private hotel which provided apartment lodgings for families.

Upper Gardens with fir plantations, 1870s. To the left of the path is the site of the present tennis courts. The large houses overlooking the gardens occupied a prime position.

The Upper Gardens and rear of houses at the eastern end of Surrey Road, built in the 1870s. The houses remain, although much altered and largely obscured from the gardens by tree growth. More obtrusive, however, is Wessex Way, which now lies uncomfortably close to the house in the foreground.

Playtime at Children's Corner, early 1900s. This part of the Lower Gardens has long provided a popular opportunity to sail miniature vessels in the Bourne Stream. In 1858 there was a plan to convey the stream in underground pipes to aid the drainage and sewage systems of the town. Fortunately for generations of children this idea was dropped, and the stream remains an attractive feature of the Gardens.

Invalids Walk, on the slopes of the Westover Pleasure Gardens, was created in 1858 to provide a quiet, sheltered promenade for sufferers from ill health. The almost continuous line of benches must have been a reassuring sight to the patient suffering from breathing difficulties, who the air of the town was said to benefit. The path was known as Invalids Walk until after the First World War when it was renamed Pine Walk.

Invalids Walk, early 1900s. The changing of the name reflected a desire to disassociate Bournemouth with disease and sickness. Although a popular place, its image was often that of a colony of respirator-wearing invalids in bath chairs. Another agreeable name change was that of Bourne Avenue, which had previously been known as Sanatorium Road.

A peaceful wooded spot in the Lower Gardens.

Winter Gardens Pavilion. The Bournemouth Winter Gardens Company hoped that their glass pavilion would provide an attraction similar to Crystal Palace. It opened in 1877, but despite fancy stalls, exhibitions and art shows it was never a great success. An improvement came in 1893 when the structure was let to Bournemouth Municipal Orchestra and rose with their reputation. However, the pavilion had not been designed as a concert hall and the orchestra moved to more suitable premises in the new Pavilion in the late 1920s. The structure was eventually dismantled in 1935.

The interior of the Winter Gardens Pavilion.

Lower Gardens, looking towards The Square, with a few people taking strolls or relaxing in the gardens. The Congregational church at the foot of Richmond Hill has been replaced with Central Chambers, erected in 1888. The lower floor was the Cadena Café and the upper floors were the Mansion Hotel, later the Empress Hotel, until just after the First World War when the whole building was taken over by National Provincial Bank. NatWest still occupy the building.

Lower Gardens, looking towards The Square, early 1900s. The gardens, with a rustic bridge over the stream, clumps of ornamental shrubbery and lighted pathways, look fairly well established.

Winter scene in the Upper Gardens. The Mont Dore Hotel, now the town hall, can be seen in the background.

Lower Gardens near the pier. The villas include Cliftonville and Brookside, which have since been incorporated into the Hermitage Hotel.

Lower Gardens and Brookside Boarding House. John Keble, famous author of *The Christian Year* and influential member of the Church of England, came to Bournemouth in 1865 because of his wife's ill health and stayed at Brookside. He died there the following year and a stained glass window was placed as a memorial in St Peter's, where he had worshipped during his stay.

Lower Gardens. The attractive rustic bridges were part of the overall garden design and replaced wooden planks which previously had been used to cross the stream.

Lower Gardens from Pier Approach, early 1900s.

Children's Corner, still providing a place for fun in the 1920s.

Rock Gardens and Pavilion, Lower Gardens. The building of the Pavilion met the need for an appropriate theatre and concert hall in Bournemouth. Before its erection there was no satisfactory entertainment venue in town, which added to the negative image of Bournemouth as a place for invalids. Plans for such a venue had been in progress since the early 1900s but the war and disputes over licensing delayed matters. The Pavilion was finally opened in 1929 by the Duke of Gloucester.

The Pavilion and Baths. The Pavilion also provided a new home for the Bournemouth Municipal Orchestra, which had previously played at the Winter Gardens Pavilion. Founded in 1893, under the direction of Dan Godfrey, the orchestra had become the first permanent one of its kind in the country. Its fame spread and as the Bournemouth Symphony Orchestra, although no longer at this venue, it is still internationally renowned today. The Corporation Baths, on the opposite side of Bath Road, were opened in 1935 and replaced Sydenham's Reading Rooms and the previous baths. The site was more recently a car park until 1998 when it returned to leisure use with the building of the Waterfront entertainment complex.

CHAPTER TWO

CHURCHES

Many of Bournemouth's town centre churches are evidence of the huge growth in the population of the town during the second half of the nineteenth century. An increased population meant a wider diversity of beliefs and the need for adequate places of worship in which to express them.

The Church of England was represented with a temporary building until the original St Peter's was built in 1843. It was small, of no great architectural significance and was perhaps inadequate even at this early stage of Bournemouth's history. Increased demand and the rising status of the town warranted the plan of extensions and improvements, which transformed St Peter's into the church of today.

Other denominations became apparent as Bournemouth grew. Presbyterians, Congregationalists and Wesleyans all started with small facilities, but with increased support and growing congregations were building and enlarging their churches during the 1850s and 1860s. The town also had to cater for more than its own population. In the season the number of churchgoers was swelled by visitors, many of whom stayed for months rather than weeks, and so expected to continue their regular pattern of worship. It was in this way that the first provision for Catholics developed when a lady visitor, finding no established church, set up her own private oratory at the Belle Vue Hotel.

Richmond Hill and the Presbyterian church from The Square, 1873. The church at the foot of Richmond Hill was erected the year before this photograph was taken. It was the second Presbyterian church on that site and was itself replaced by St Andrew's, Exeter Road, in 1887. Central Chambers, now NatWest Bank, was built on the site. It can be seen from the tree growth that the rest of Richmond Hill was largely undeveloped at this time.

The spire of St Andrew's Presbyterian church dominates this view, looking towards The Square from the Lower Gardens. The church was built in 1887 and is still there, although without the spire, which was dismantled in 1947 after it became unsafe because of wartime bombing.

The interior of St Andrew's Presbyterian church.

St Peter's, 1870s. The church is the final resting place of a well-known literary family: Sir Percy Florence Shelley lived at Boscombe Manor from the 1850s. He lies in a tomb at St Peter's with his mother, Mary Shelley, author of *Frankenstein*. His father, Percy Bysshe Shelley, the romantic thinker and poet, had died by drowning off the Italian coast years earlier. Although his ashes are buried in Rome, his heart lies with Mary at St Peter's.

St Peter's, from Hinton Road, 1870s. St Peter's was built over a period spanning thirty years, during which well-planned additions were made to the original structure. The tower was added in 1869 but had to wait another ten years before it was topped by the spire. The characteristic lych gate in this view will be a familiar site to all those who have awaited a bus (or in this case a horse-drawn carriage) in its shade.

St Peter's from Gervis Place, complete with spire, the vane of which is over 200 ft from the ground.

The Roman Catholic church in Richmond Hill, on the corner of Albert Road. Built in 1874 to serve the growing number of Catholics in the town, it was much enlarged during the 1890s. The church is no longer so apparent in Richmond Hill because buildings of a similar height now surround it. The house to the left of the church was replaced by the *Echo* building in the 1930s.

The spire of Richmond Hill Congregational church overlooking the attractive Upper Gardens just before the First World War. Built in 1890, this church replaced an original structure of the late 1850s.

The interior of Richmond Hill Congregational church. One of the best known Congregationalist preachers was the Revd John Daniel Jones, who was at Richmond Hill for nearly forty years until his retirement in 1937.

East Cliff Congregational church. In 1877 twenty-seven members of the Richmond Hill Congregational church left to form this new church on Holdenhurst Road.

Holy Trinity church, Old Christchurch Road. The tower of Holy Trinity, which dwarfs the surrounding commercial buildings, was added to the church in 1878. One hundred years later it was destroyed by fire and the church demolished.

CHAPTER THREE
CLIFFS & SANDS

The sands and sea at Bournemouth were seen as one of the town's prime attractions. Sea water was said to cure a range of common ailments. Bathing was considered beneficial from a medical point of view and it was recommended that quick plunges before noon followed by a brisk rub down would do the most good. The concept of bathing, however, also caused alarm to many Victorians. In the early days men bathed in the nude and ladies often followed suit. Blushes were supposed to be spared by segregated beaches and the use of bathing machines whereby you could immerse yourself totally before the machine was pulled away. In practice, however, it would seem that exhibitionists and the curious managed to shock or be shocked on numerous occasions. It would also seem that this liberated feeling was perhaps rather refreshing to the upright Victorians. Even Bournemouth, beloved by the sick and elderly, was witness to the worrying trend of exposure of the flesh. Indeed, one contemporary account states: 'visitors to Bournemouth are more shameless than at any other place'.

Incredibly, it was also recommended that sea water be taken internally. A glass or two followed by some beer or gin, followed in most cases – and not surprisingly – by vomiting, was said by some to be highly beneficial.

Soon the benefits of sea air became as important as the actual water, and Bournemouth's climate was hailed as a prime example, warm and softened as it was by the scent of pine trees.

Apart from bathing from the sands, Bournemouth beach also held attractions for the growing Victorian hobby of natural history study and collection. The flora, fauna and geology of the chines, cliffs and shore provided a happy hunting ground for the enthusiastic naturalist.

View from West Cliff, 1870s. This early view shows how natural and rugged the cliffs were at this time. An early Bournemouth guide book draws attention in its narrative to the lack of paths on the cliff summit and laments the fact that, owing to this, ladies are only able to view the scenery from the bottom of the cliffs.

East Cliff Sands, 1880s. The long stretch of golden sand at Bournemouth was seen as a great advantage to those who wished to bathe in the open sea. As can be seen from this view, Victorian adults made little adjustment in their dress for a walk on the sands. Children were permitted to paddle, but adult bathers made use of the portable bathing machines to save their dignity when entering the water.

View from East Cliff, 1870s. A path did exist from the pier entrance, up past the cliff frontage of the Bath Hotel to join East Cliff Road, but beyond this the footpath petered out and the land became dominated by sandhills until the approach to Boscombe.

West Cliff, 1890s. Considering the style of dress that ladies were expected to wear, it is not surprising that they were unable to appreciate the cliff top views until suitable paths were

laid. From the cliff top, spectacular views of Hengistbury Head, the Isle of Wight and the Purbeck Hills must have gone some way towards compensating for what must have been a hot and uncomfortable ascent in such elaborate attire.

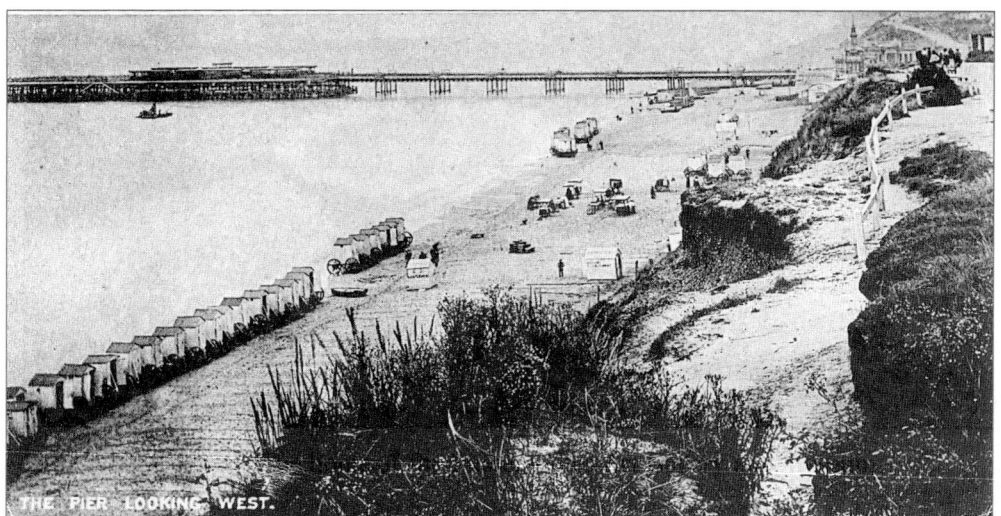

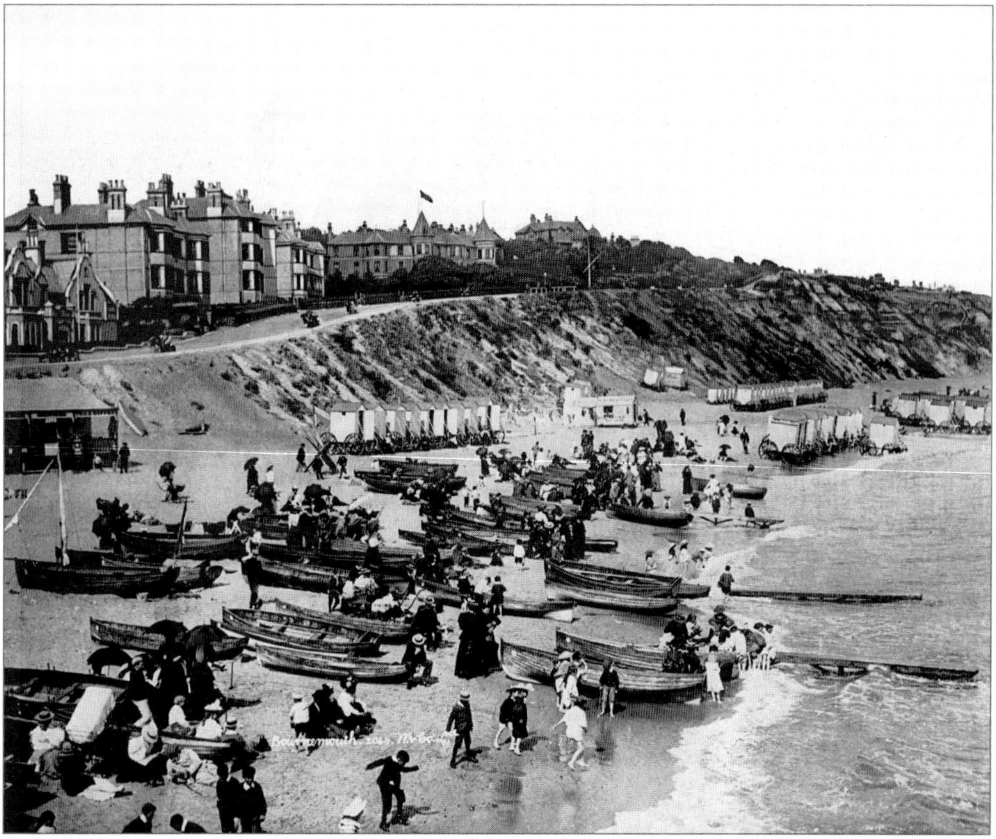
Bournemouth

East Cliff Sands, 1890s. Rowing boats and bathing machines clutter the beach in this view. The small hut on the sands is that of A. Roberts and Co. The lettering on the front reads 'All Bathers Pay Here' and refers to the hire of bathing machines.

THE PIER LOOKING WEST.

East Cliff Sands, 1890s. An early Bournemouth guide book voices the opinion that although bathing machines were neatly constructed, their sheer number and conspicuousness could spoil the picturesque appearance of the seaside.

East Cliff Sands, 1890s. Before Undercliff Drive was constructed, few people would have ventured too far from the pier area.

East Cliff, 1890s. As can be seen in this view, efforts were made to improve the safety and accessibility of the cliffs for visitors.

East Cliff zigzag path. The various zigzag paths on the Bournemouth cliffs greatly improved their accessibility to visitors, although no doubt they were too much for invalids. At this time the cliff face was largely barren and so the rugged nature of the cliffs was more apparent.

Children having fun with the tide and a raft early this century.

Various shelters soon appeared on the cliff tops for the benefit of those who appreciated the breathtaking views but didn't care so much for the strong winds.

The Beach, *c.* 1905. An interesting study of relaxed holidaymakers on the sands next to the pier.

West Cliff Sands. The Undercliff Drive west of the pier was opened in 1911. This changed the look of the cliff face, with refreshment rooms and beach huts established at the bottom of the cliff.

The Pines, West Cliff, Bournemouth

Pines at West Cliff, *c.* 1917. The first landowners in Bournemouth created many plantations of pine tree, replacing much of the native gorse and sandy heathland. At first they planted Scots Pine but soon found that Maritime Pine was more suitable. It was this variety that formed the majority of plantings and the species was so abundant that it soon became known as the Bournemouth Pine. Although the loss of the natural landscape was not to everyone's taste, the pines did help in establishing Bournemouth's reputation as a health resort. Their presence was said to soften the climate and improve the quality of the air.

The West Cliff in particular was noted for its changing height and form. Interested visitors to early Bournemouth also had the pleasure of exploring the various chines, which were left in a relatively natural state for some years.

East Cliff Sands, *c*. 1918. This view was taken after the construction of the Undercliff Drive. Bathing machines are no longer so much in evidence and a line of static beach huts has appeared at the base of the cliff. East Cliff Hall, the home of Merton and Annie Russell-Cotes, can be seen commanding splendid views from the cliff top.

Two ladies sunning themselves on West Cliff Sands. The gradual adoption of special bathing wear reflected how society became more comfortable with allowing relaxation and enjoyment of a day on the beach.

The beach, 1930s. A dense crowd has gathered on the beach and it shows a completely different scene to the Victorian views. On the West Cliff, apart from a few buildings on the extreme left of the view, everything has been replaced by the Bournemouth International Centre. The BIC plays host to a variety of comedy and music events, competitions and conferences.

CHAPTER FOUR
TRANSPORT

The development of transport in Bournemouth has followed industrial and technological progress. Events such as the nationwide coming of the railways and the invention of the internal combustion engine have all had a direct effect on the growth and success of Bournemouth as a seaside destination and a place to live and work.

The role of the town as a holiday resort, rather than an industrial centre, led to the use of transport for entertainment value as opposed to heavy labour or the transportation of goods. Excursions to nearby places of interest, taking London visitors to see the Rufus Stone in the New Forest or the cove at Lulworth, for example, meant horse carriages and charabancs. A fleet of steamships ferried people on day trips to places such as the Isle of Wight or Swanage.

A public transport system, perhaps more important to the town's permanent occupants, has also been developed over the years by the Corporation. Various forms of public conveyance have had their heyday but have been replaced as technology has progressed.

East Cliff Lift and bath chair. Bath chairs were very popular at Victorian seaside resorts, as they were ideal for conveying ladies and invalids. Bath chairs could be pushed from behind but the steering was operated by the occupant. The chair in this view is drawn by two donkeys.

Coach and horses at The Square. Until 1870 there was no railway at Bournemouth and visitors had to reach the town by some other method. One of the nearest railway stations was Hamworthy near Poole from where a coach could be hired for the remainder of the journey.

Aboard the *Emperor of India*, 1913. This steamer, belonging to Messrs Cosens and Co., had been working for five years at the date of this photograph. The following year the happy holidaymakers would be gone, as she was requisitioned for war service.

Brodick Castle was purchased by the Bournemouth, Poole and Swanage Steam Packet Company in 1887. In 1908 she was sold to Messrs Cosens and Co., but in 1909 they decided to sell her for use as a cattle boat in the Argentine. The following year, while being towed to her new life, she sank off the coast at Portland.

Aboard the *Bournemouth Queen*, 1934. Steamships had called at the pier since the early 1860s but it was not until 1869 that the first company was established to provide excursions from Bournemouth. In the years that followed, trips on the various steamers became one of the most popular recreational activities at the resort. *Bournemouth Queen* belonged to the Southampton, Isle of Wight and South Coast Steam Packet Company and made her first voyage in July 1908. Six years later she was to be engaged for service in the war as a minesweeper and patrol vessel. In the Second World War she acted as an anti-aircraft ship. She continued in the pleasure trade until 1957 when she was towed to Belgium for breaking up.

Aboard the *Monarch*, 1935. The *Monarch* belonged to Messrs Cosens and Co., and did local and cross Channel trips for just over sixty years, from 1888 to 1950, making her an extremely popular and well-known ship. Her war service years were spent as a minesweeper in the Bristol and Irish Channels.

Bournemouth Corporation tram, no. 6, *c.* 1900. The Corporation had disagreements with another company for a few years over the running of a tram system until the Bournemouth Corporation Tramways Act in 1903 settled matters and gave the Corporation responsibility for running a service between Christchurch and Poole. This tram is about to leave the Lansdowne and set off down Christchurch Road towards Boscombe. The line from the Lansdowne to Pokesdown was opened in 1902.

A Bournemouth Corporation tram.

First Sunday tram to Winton, 1913. There had been controversy surrounding the decision of whether or not to allow a Sunday tram service in the town. The Corporation made their final decision by polling the town's rate payers, who were marginally in favour of a Sunday service by around 500 votes. Trams had been running to Winton since 1903, when an expensive system was installed to pull the trams up the steep gradient of Richmond Hill.

Horse coach, 1913. These people are about to leave for a trip around the New Forest.

Charabanc at The Square, 1913. These motorised carriages provided an alternative to horse-drawn vehicles for an excursion to the local beauty spots.

Charabanc outside Sydenham's, Pier Approach. Hundreds of these day excursions took place during the summer season, and there was usually a photographer around to capture the occasion as a souvenir.

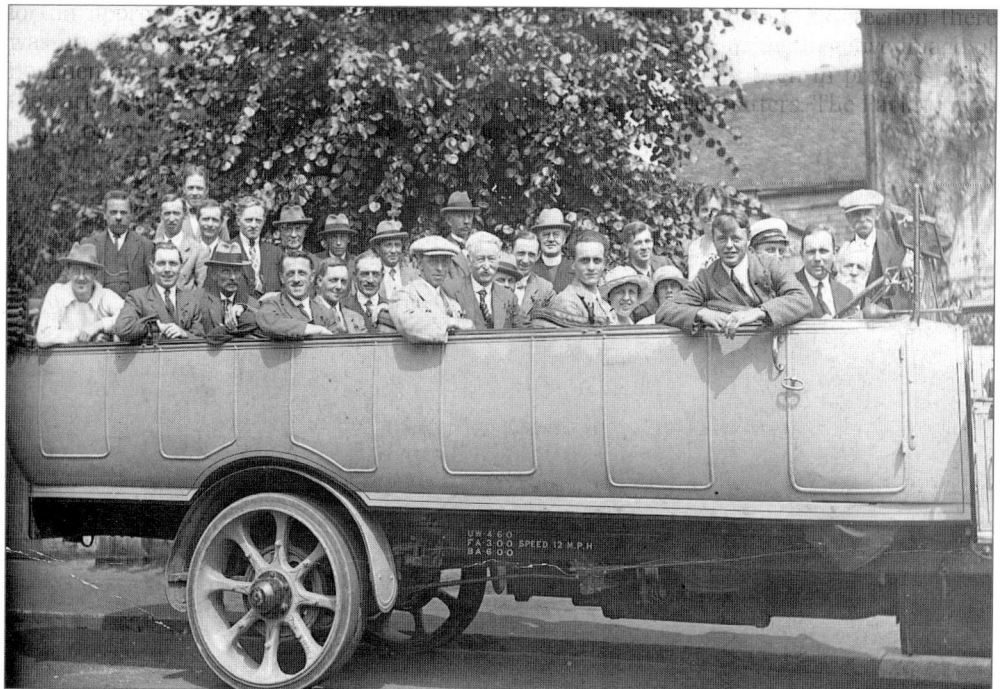

Although this was not a speedy way to reach your destination, the fact that so many friends and family could be fitted into one car must have ensured a good day out.

A view of congested Bournemouth transport. Four different forms of transport can be seen: car, tram, bicycle and trolley-bus. The operation of a trolley-bus service was implemented after the Bournemouth Corporation Act of 1930 made provision for an experimental scheme. The pilot routes were a success and in time trolley-buses took over from trams entirely. Now, of course, they have themselves been replaced.

CHAPTER FIVE

CENTRAL
BOURNEMOUTH
& THE SQUARE

The area known as The Square, an open space between the two principal shopping areas of Commercial Road and Old Christchurch Road, has undergone gradual expansion in size as Bournemouth has developed. The area was first called The Bridge, simply because that's what it was – a small bridge over the River Bourne. The gardens abutted either side and the area was no wider than the width of the road. Successive widenings over the years meant that it became less obvious as a bridge, particularly after remodelling of the area in 1899 when the stone balustrades were removed. This development also expanded the area to include half an acre of the gardens, and a circular island was constructed in the centre.

The area was first referred to as The Square in 1858. Considering that the name has never matched the shape of the area, it is assumed that the new town of Bournemouth was following the tradition of ancient market towns in designating this central open space as a square. However, this did cause confusion, and some early visitors to Bournemouth were so misled they called for The Square to be renamed.

The Square, 1890s. The buildings on the curve of Exeter Road and Commercial Road are sited where the Moon on the Square pub and Debenhams are now. The billboard near the bridge is advertising a Grand Evening Concert.

This balustrade is part of the bridge over the Bourne Stream in The Square. Before the trees were fully grown, the photographer had an uninterrupted view along the Upper Gardens.

This view looks towards Lower Gardens and the sea. A variety of vehicles line Bourne Avenue, whereas the opposite side is dense tree growth. Again, this view shows clearly how the Bourne Stream was crossed by the bridge and the gardens came right up to the road. With each successive road widening a little more of the gardens has been lost. On the left there is a building under construction.

An unfamiliar part of Bournemouth, with a spire-less St Peter's, 1870s.

This view is from the top of Braidley Road with Meyrick Park to the right of the view. The area was soon used to build Victorian villas, and the continued housing demand means that some have been replaced by modern flats. It is difficult to imagine now that the area was once used for grazing.

Gervis Place, with the Arcade on the left and St Peter's church.

An unusual view, looking along Bath Road where it runs almost parallel to the sea. The white building in the centre of the photograph is the side elevation of the Belle Vue Hotel. The large detached villas in the background are those in Exeter Lane which face on to the Lower Gardens.

The Richmond Hill area, 1870s.

From Richmond Hill, 1870. This view looks towards Exeter and Commercial Roads, situated where Debenhams is now.

Near the pier, 1920s. The sign on the left is advertising the building of the new Pavilion by Jones and Seward Ltd, Building Contractors. The demolition of the Belle Vue Hotel on this site and the erection of the Pavilion greatly altered this part of Bournemouth.

Portman Lodge (see also p. 69). This cottage was built in 1811 by Captain Tregonwell for his butler to live in. Tregonwell himself lived further up Exeter Road in a mansion which now forms part of the Royal Exeter Hotel. Before it burnt down in 1922, Portman Lodge was a favourite subject for photographers as it was so picturesque and often laid claim to being the oldest house in Bournemouth. After the fire it was mostly rebuilt but was unfortunately demolished a few years later. It was replaced by the Hants and Dorset Bus Station, which has also since vanished from the site.

The Square, c. 1905, looking up Richmond Hill with the spire of the Punshon Memorial church visible – just behind the Central Hotel. Both the church and the hotel were bombed in 1943 and had to be demolished; the Empress Hotel and Central Chambers at the foot of the hill remained largely undamaged. The building on the opposite side is Richmond Chambers.

The Square, *c.* 1906. The Square underwent much development from the 1880s onwards. The Presbyterian church at the foot of Richmond Hill was demolished and replaced by Central Chambers and the Empress Hotel. In this view, it can be seen how the central area has widened considerably from earlier photographs. The circular centrepiece which introduced a focal point to The Square was added in the late 1890s.

Entrance to the Lower Gardens, *c.* 1926.

The Square, looking towards Old Christchurch Road and Gervis Place, mid-1920s. The Square was remodelled in 1925 and the centrepiece made more noticeable, with the addition of a clock and shelter structure. Trams were now running through The Square and the shops were attracting visitors.

The Square, looking towards Old Christchurch Road and Gervis Place, early 1930s: a similar view to the previous one, although the skyline is altered with the Pavilion roof clearly visible. Another major development is that Richmond Chambers has been replaced by a bigger building, although still for the old firm of Hankinson and Son.

The Square, looking from Exeter Road towards Bourne Avenue, *c.* 1947. Now a busy pedestrianised area, The Square retains its characteristic clock tower, perhaps now a little isolated as the enclosing structure has been removed. The buildings lining Bourne Avenue have changed little in appearance since this photograph, although their function and occupiers have. The spire belongs to Richmond Hill Congregational church and is still a noticeable feature in the same view today.

The Square, 1873. This view looks across The Square towards Old Christchurch Road and the parade of shops known as Southbourne Terrace. The Presbyterian church is at the foot of Richmond Hill. The leisurely attitude of the people in this view may be largely for the benefit of the camera, but The Square was still in its infancy and was undoubtedly a fairly quiet and uncrowded place at this time. The balustrades of the bridge over the Bourne Stream can clearly be seen. It was this area which gradually widened over the years to become the large open space we associate with The Square today. The following two images show how The Square altered over the years.

The Square, *c.* 1905.

The Square, 1920s.

The Square, *c.* 1936.

Central Bournemouth, 1872. St Peter's church and Southbourne Terrace in Old Christchurch Road are recognisable features of this view. The attractive thatched cottage is Portman Lodge, which was located approximately where the NCP car park at Exeter Crescent is now.

A similar view, although St Peter's is now even more commanding over the town. The unusual spire in the background is that of Holy Trinity church in Old Christchurch Road. Before the building of tall flats and office blocks, the spires of the various churches were unmissable in the skyline.

CHAPTER SIX

SHOPS

As with churches, the increase in the number of shops in Bournemouth was related to the growth in the town's population. In the early stages it was necessary to take a trip to Poole if anything was required. Gradually establishments opened in Commercial Road and around The Square, which is still the hub of Bournemouth's shopping area. On the opposite side of The Square, the building of Southbourne Terrace and the Arcade established commerce in Old Christchurch Road.

The Square, 1890s. Exeter Road is on the left with Commercial Road leading away to the right. T.J. Hankinson on the far left was a stationer, publisher and estate agent, and also provided a library and pianofortes for hire! The site is now occupied by the Moon on the Square pub.

Southbourne Terrace and Rebbeck's from the Lower Gardens. Southbourne Terrace was completed in 1865 and comprised six shops with three storeys of domestic accommodation above. Today, the first three shops have been amalgamated as W.H. Smith. The others remain as individual premises and are largely unchanged above the shop frontage. The small building on the right is Rebbeck's estate agents on the corner of Old Christchurch Road and Gervis Place. Rebbeck's remained here until the 1930s, when they relocated and larger premises were erected on this corner plot.

Beale's, Old Christchurch Road. John Elmes Beale's first commercial venture in Bournemouth was a small fancy fair which he opened in 1881. His business expanded over the years and in 1912 this five-storey department store was opened. Beale was well known for his publicity stunts; in 1913 it was arranged for the store's Father Christmas to arrive by aeroplane! This building was destroyed by an air raid in 1943 but Beale's still occupies the site in a new building dating from the early 1950s.

The Arcade, early 1870s. Henry Joy began building the Arcade, first known as Gervis Arcade, in 1866. This photograph was taken before the Arcade was roofed over in 1872 and before development took place on either side. The first occupants included Sarah Kempster, confectioner; Robert Savoin, auctioneer; and Edward Offer, tobacconist at no. 6. Offer's brass sign can still be seen in the present shop front.

Once covered, the Arcade became highly popular as a shopping centre. Its success led to similar developments in neighbouring Westbourne and Boscombe.

A.G. Simpson's dispensing pharmacy, with its remarkable array of jars and bottles, was at Bank Buildings in Boscombe.

Worlds Stores, Bournemouth.

CHAPTER SEVEN

THE PIER

By the beginning of the twentieth century piers were a characteristic sight of the typically English seaside resort and were known for their cheap and cheerful entertainment value. The pier's more practical origin was to provide a landing stage for ships at coastal towns where there was no natural harbour. In time they became attractions and towns that built piers found that they led to a boost in visitor numbers. It was approaching the state where the presence of a pier was one of the criteria for defining a holiday resort.

Bournemouth was relatively late in achieving such a desirable attraction. A jetty was constructed in 1855 but the need for bigger and better was recognised. The Bournemouth Improvement Act of 1856 stated that a pier must be built within five years.

The resulting structure was designed by the well-known engineer George Rennie, and cost £3,418. Construction was hampered and delayed by disagreements, bad weather and financial problems but the pier was finally opened in 1861 by Sir George Gervis. It lasted less than twenty years. The pier's wooden construction suffered an attack of toredo worm, and it was badly damaged by two destructive storms.

By 1878 it was evident that a new pier was needed. Around this time pier construction was changing, because of advances in marine engineering and innovative uses of ironwork. Many piers around the country were extended, and elaborate ironwork façades were added to disguise the iron and wood structure underneath.

This trend can be traced in Bournemouth's second pier, which was designed by engineer Eugenius Birch and opened in 1880. Built of iron, it was of a more elaborate and decorative style than its predecessor and deliberately set out to attract and make money from holidaymakers.

The pier was closed for the duration of the Second World War. Post-war reconstruction swept away the Victorian style and replaced it with a modern 1950s pierhead, although its attraction to visitors remains.

A view from the pier, 1860s. The first of Bournemouth's piers, opened in 1861 to replace the previous jetty, was 1,000 ft long and 15 ft wide, although its length was shortened after damaging storms in 1867 and 1876. It looks to have been a fairly simple structure, with just a few shelters and standard lamps for the benefit of visitors. The Belle Vue Hotel can be seen on the right.

Pier entrance from West Cliff, 1860s. This view shows the simple entrance to the first pier. Its functional and unpretentious design can be contrasted with the style of its successor.

Pier entrance from West Cliff, 1880s. The new pier entrance housed resting areas, lavatories and waiting rooms for both ladies and gentlemen. It made use of pitch pine, plate glass, majolica panels and decorative paintwork to create an elaborate environment.

Compared with the similar view of the first pier, it is obvious how the second pier was superior in providing an attractive promenade for visitors. It boasted an ornamental side rail, seating for 1,000 people and glass shelter boxes, all lit up at night by sixty globular lamps.

The pier from East Cliff, early 1880s. The second pier stretched for a total of 838 ft. It was wider for the final 188 ft to allow for a landing stage for steamers.

Pier entrance, 1880s. The impressive clock tower was added to the pier entrance in 1882, the clock being a gift from Mr Horace Davey, parliamentary representative for Bournemouth.

View from the pier, *c.* 1900. The Bournemouth Commissioners must have been grateful for the success of their new pier. As well as being an added attraction, the pier provided a good source of revenue for them – as there was an entrance charge.

The pier from East Cliff. The covered shelters and bandstand at the pier head were added in 1885. Brass bands were extremely popular forms of seaside entertainment. Before regulations were adopted, the noise of itinerant bands competing for audiences could make the seafront a less than peaceful place.

Pier Approach. The extremely ornate construction of the pier entrance, a style which Victorians craved, can be clearly seen in this view. From the pier entrance bath chairs and bathing machines could be hired.

The pier from East Cliff. The design of the entrance is mirrored in the elegant structure of the pier itself.

The entrance to Undercliff Drive, the first section of which opened in 1911, can be seen in this view. The first plan for such a drive had been in 1878 but opinions differed and any attempts at positive action had failed to reach a conclusion. It wasn't until the new century that a serious step was taken, and a deputation of Bournemouth Commissioners visited similar sites both here and on the continent to help them plan an Undercliff Drive for their own town.

Servicemen enjoying their leave during the First World War.

Pier Approach, *c*. 1924. The building of the Undercliff Drive undoubtedly pleased the growing enthusiasts of the motor car. As today, it provided an ideal stretch of road on which to cruise along the seafront to the admiring and envious gaze of others.

Pier entrance, 1940s. A new look for the pier entrance swept away the Victorian fussiness at a time when Victorian attitudes, particularly regarding appropriate seaside behaviour, were being challenged and changed.

CHAPTER EIGHT
EVENTS

Events in Bournemouth have encompassed celebrations, entertainment, marking of occasions, crisis and wartime. Some events may have been deliberately aimed at the summer visitor, but the church parades and outings of various clubs, professions and societies proves that Bournemouth residents had their own individuality and sense of tradition.

Despite Bournemouth being a modern town, its occupants were still keen on established ceremony. Its rapid growth and development ensured a regular programme of openings involving civic dignitaries, speeches, pride in the town and usually a lavish teatime spread afterwards.

Perhaps the most ambitious event of the past was the Bournemouth Centenary Fêtes of 1910, when the whole town could not help but be involved in the celebrations.

The Boscombe Whale, 1897. The whale was washed up on the beach near Boscombe Pier and for a couple of years its skeleton was exhibited on the pier as a major attraction.

An outing for Boscombe Working Men's Conservative Club, 1908. It would appear that none of them wanted to ride inside the carriage.

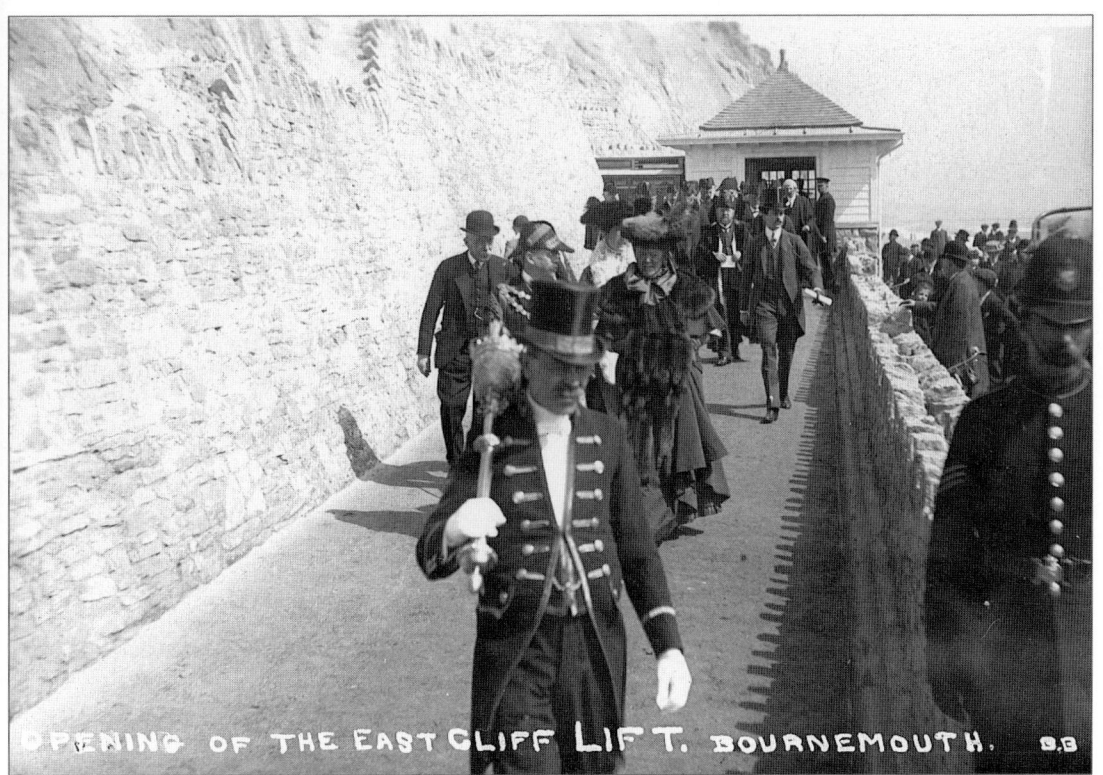

OPENING OF THE EAST CLIFF LIFT. BOURNEMOUTH.

The opening of East Cliff Lift, 1908. The mace-bearer precedes the opening party of Sir George and Lady Meyrick and the Mayor of Bournemouth, G.E. Bridge.

East Cliff Lift, 1908. The lift has just opened in this view and is drawing the attention of quite a crowd, both above and below. The enterprising photographer is determined to get a good shot. The cable lift was to save the precious energy of the invalid and elderly, a task it still performs ninety years on.

OPENING OF BOURNEMOUTH PIER EXTENSION by THE LORD MAYOR of LONDON

The opening of the pier extension, 1909. This event drew large crowds and an impressive line of dignitaries to perform the ceremony.

POSTMEN'S CHURCH PARADE BOURNEMOUTH 24.4.10

Postmen's Church Parade, 1910. This procession of smartly uniformed postmen is marching its way round the Lansdowne with the Hotel Metropole in the background.

Bournemouth Centenary Fêtes, 1910: the arrival of the Lord Mayor of London. In 1810 Captain L.D.G. Tregonwell had bought his first plot of land in Bournemouth from Sir George Tapps, on which he built his home. As Tregonwell was seen as the founder of Bournemouth,

ntenary Fetes,
d Mayor of London's Arrival

this year was marked as the beginning of the modern town. One hundred years later the
lavish Centenary Fêtes were organised to mark the occasion.

Much of the programme consisted of carnival processions. The organisers were hoping for scenes and an atmosphere similar to the elaborate and 'grotesque' fêtes that drew the crowds on the French Riviera. They even employed French designers to produce the characters and figures.

These people are taking part in one of the two Battle of Flowers processions where prizes were awarded to decorated cars. Lady Wimborne won first prize in the second procession; her car was decorated with hydrangeas.

Bournemouth Centenary Fetes,
Old Christchurch Rd

A procession along Old Christchurch Road during the Centenary Fêtes. As can be seen in this view, for ten days in July the whole town was decked out with ribbons, bunting, flags and banners. No expense was spared, to the extent that the Fêtes Committee failed to cover their expenditure with receipts. However, as a publicity event, the fêtes were an undoubted success. Such colourful scenes of rejoicing must have gone a long way to burying the staid and stuffy image from which the town had suffered. The spectacle of a town so lavishly celebrating its first 100 years increased Bournemouth's popularity and renown worldwide.

International Aviation Meeting, 1910. 'Dickson in Flight.' Perhaps because Bournemouth was relatively new the town chose to link itself to the latest advance in transportation, namely flying. The Centenary Fêtes deliberately coincided with the International Aviation Meeting, with competitions and demonstration flights to add to the excitement of the celebrations.

'Christaens Starting a Flight.' The special aerodrome created for the event was at Southbourne. This was the first time that the meeting had been held in this country, and it must have made the Bournemouth Commissioners and Fête Committee swell with pride that Bournemouth was chosen to host such a prestigious event.

'The Hon. C. Rolls Rising for a Flight.' Tragically, the meeting was also the occasion of the first fatal accident involving a British pilot. On Tuesday 12 July the Hon. Charles Stewart Rolls died while competing in the Alighting Competition. The tail of his Short-Wright biplane snapped as he was attempting to land on a marked spot.

'Barnes Preparing for a Flight', 1910. Bournemouth maintained its interest in aviation after this event. In 1914 Gustav Hamel broke the 'loop the loop' record over Meyrick Park. Later, in 1919, the prestigious Schneider trophy was competed for at Bournemouth.

A parade in Hinton Road. The crowd looks expectant but sombre and there are no flags or bunting, suggesting a rather solemn reason for this event.

The civic opening of a section of the eagerly awaited Undercliff Drive.

Foresters Church Parade, 1914.

Recruiting March at Bournemouth, April 1915. Before conscription, recruiting marches and meetings could double the number of men volunteering for service.

1st Convoy passing through Bournemouth, August 1914. The convoy is passing in front of Richmond Chambers at the foot of Richmond Hill.

A crowd of holidaymakers in Bournemouth Gardens, 1923. They were probably awaiting the start of a concert in the Lower Gardens.

CHAPTER NINE
HOTELS

In the early days of Bournemouth's development, hotels were not necessarily needed to attract visitors. The people able to afford the time and money to travel to Bournemouth, in order to get away from the bustle of London or for the sake of their health, were likely to stay upwards of a month or for the whole season. Such lengthy stays warranted all the comforts of home so it was preferable to rent a newly built mansion or villa and, in effect, bring the household with them. Maids, nannies, cooks, butlers and coachmen would all follow the family to Bournemouth and perform their usual routines to keep the household running efficiently and the family members in comfort.

Hotels did exist, such as the Royal Bath and the Belle Vue, but it wasn't until the 1870s and '80s that hotel building really took off. This was as a result of improved access to Bournemouth. The railway meant that shorter stays were feasible, although still for the more wealthy visitor. This period saw the construction of many vast establishments, often with health facilities to attract the wealthy sick and elderly who were impressed by stories of the healing Bournemouth air. Compared with older towns, where accommodation was in ancient coaching inns, these new hotels were large, clean, modern and exciting. Most of the large hotels played host to famous authors, actors and European royalty. Unfortunately many of these hotels have since lost their original splendour or never recovered from wartime requisitioning. Others have been demolished to make way for flats or more modern hotels.

During the twentieth century innovations in transport and the provision for time off work and paid holidays meant that seaside resorts attracted a growing number of people from all social levels. This is reflected in the rise of small, family run lodgings and boarding houses. These were often converted houses and sprung up mainly in the sides streets of Bournemouth and Boscombe. By the 1950s most tastes and pockets could be catered for in the vast range of accommodation available.

The Bath Hotel was opened by Sir George Gervis on the day of Queen Victoria's coronation in 1838. This early view shows the coaches that were used to ferry guests to and from the nearest railway stations at Poole. It was the main hotel in Bournemouth for many years. In 1876 it was bought by Merton Russell-Cotes, who extended the hotel and reopened it in 1880. As the Royal Bath Hotel it was a huge success, and the way in which the Russell-Cotes used the rooms to display their collection of treasures from around the world helped to establish the reputation and fame of the hotel. The front entrance is still recognisable today.

The Belle Vue Hotel, 1920s. The Belle Vue was built as a boarding house in 1838 and provided some of the first accommodation for visitors to Bournemouth. Its situation, where the Pavilion now stands, was ideally close to the sands and the pier. The Belle Vue also offered a library and the assembly rooms provided the venue for meetings. It was demolished to make way for the Pavilion in 1928.

Mont Dore Hotel, *c.* 1900. Adhering to the view of Bournemouth as a health resort, this hotel was named after Mont Dore in the south of France where the waters are reputed to heal the sick. The enterprising owners had the idea of importing the water to Bournemouth and offering exclusive treatments at the Mont Dore Hotel. After opening in 1885, the hotel boasted luxurious accommodation with 120 rooms for visitors, including a dining room, reading room, billiard rooms, an 80 ft long ballroom and a special suite of rooms for royalty, all heated by steam and lit by gas. Special rooms were also built for the Mont Dore treatment – such methods as nasal and throat irrigations were on offer to the health-obsessed Victorian. Its life as a splendid hotel lasted only forty years. During the First World War the hotel was used as a military hospital. In 1920 Bournemouth Council bought the building for £33,000 for conversion to a town hall.

Boscombe Chine Hotel. Boscombe, with its spa and gardens, became as attractive to visitors as central Bournemouth. The Chine Hotel, on the cliff to the west of Boscombe Pier, provided luxurious accommodation. This sprawling building began life as the Spa Hotel in 1874. At that time the hotel comprised just the central section in this view. Over the years, as Boscombe's popularity grew, elaborate wings were added, with large windows to take maximum advantage of the spectacular views out to sea.

The Imperial Hotel occupied one of the sites at the Lansdowne. It was opened in 1888 at the junction of Bath and Meyrick Roads, where the Round House Hotel now stands.

The sprawling Grand Hotel began life as The Firs, a private house set in a large estate. In 1882 the Grand Fir Vale Hotel, an adaptation of the original house, opened. A road had also been created through the grounds – Fir Vale Road. Within a few years the hotel was known as the Grand, so it is only the road name which now links the area with the original house.

Linden Hall Hydro. Linden Hall developed from a private house overlooking Boscombe Gardens. By 1903 houses either side of the original building had been absorbed into the Hydro; it was renamed Linden Hall Hydro, and offered a variety of different baths including Turkish, Russian and medical. In 1934 a swimming pool and sports stadium were added. The building was requisitioned during the Second World War and afterwards was reopened as an hotel. In 1985 it was demolished and replaced by a block of flats named Linden Hall.

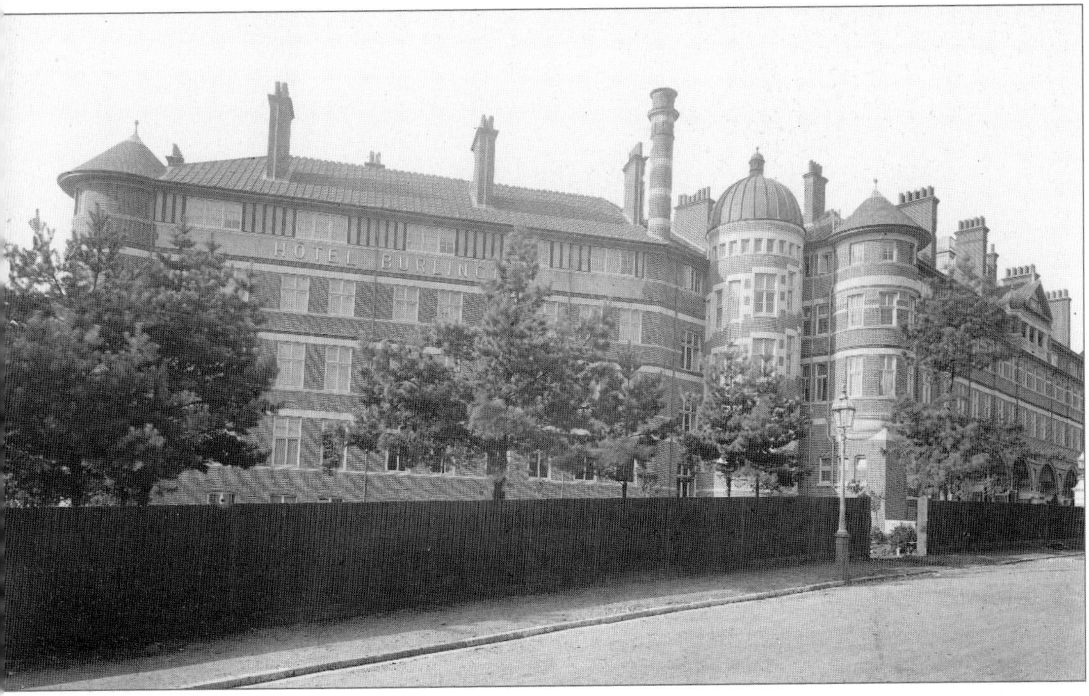
HOTEL BURLING

The Hotel Burlington opened in 1892 offering accommodation comprising 180 bedrooms and 13 suites. During the Second World War it was used as an RAF officer training centre. After the war it resumed life as an hotel, but during the late 1950s there were various plans to turn it into flats, a shopping centre or old people's home. Today it is one of the hotels that has survived.

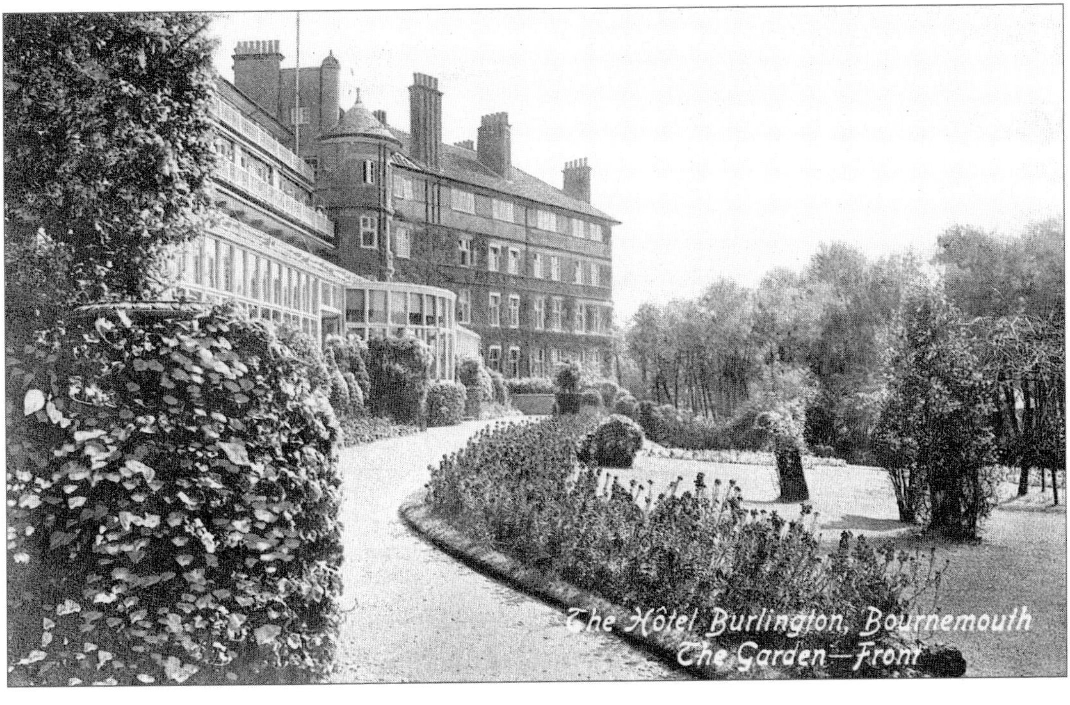
The Hôtel Burlington, Bournemouth
The Garden—Front

Ingleside Boarding Establishment, *c.* 1925. During the early twentieth century many boarding houses such as the Ingleside were established to provide alternative accommodation to the large hotels and to satisfy the increasing amount of visitors with more modest means. Most of these still exist, sometimes little changed over the years.

CHAPTER TEN

BOSCOMBE

Although not the only neighbourhood to develop as a result of Bournemouth's growth, Boscombe had the advantage of its coastal position and so could establish itself as a complementary resort.

Most building development took place from the 1870s on the stretch of barren land between Bournemouth and a small cluster of habitation at Pokesdown. Various large estates existed, such as the 174 acres on the seaward side of Christchurch Road, which was purchased by Sir Percy Florence Shelley in 1850. The existing house on the estate was rebuilt to cater for Sir Percy's cultural lifestyle: it included a private theatre, and became known as Boscombe Manor.

By the early twentieth century the northern side of Christchurch Road had been developed with more modest housing. Shops and entertainment facilities were established on either side of the main road and churches were built. The seafront had also undergone major development to provide the facilities which had now, as at Bournemouth, come to be expected by holidaymakers.

Boscombe Chine, late 1860s. This remarkable view shows the area before any development had taken place.

Boscombe Chine Gardens. The chine area, from Christchurch Road to the sea, was acquired by the Bournemouth Corporation in the 1870s and '80s. The chine was bridged and the area laid out as pleasure gardens with paths, lawns, flower beds, croquet grounds and a lodge alongside the Christchurch Road entrance.

The original Boscombe Chine bridge, 1870s.

Boscombe Spa Hotel and the Boscombe spa. The spa was a natural mineral water spring. It was enclosed and given a thatched shelter for the benefit of visitors who came to sample the water's health-giving properties.

Chine Gardens. Today these slopes are thick with tall pines and the underlying nature of the landscape is not so easy to discern.

Boscombe Pier was built as a private enterprise by the Boscombe Pier Company Ltd at a cost of £12,000; it was opened in 1889. The presence of its own pier helped to identify Boscombe as a separate entity and increased its appeal to visitors.

Skating on hired roller skates was just one of the many diversions available on the pier to keep people amused and spending money.

Christchurch Road, Boscombe. This view was taken near the entrance to Sea Road and looks towards Bournemouth. The Salisbury Hotel, on the right, was situated on the corner of Palmerston Road. Built in 1890, it provided top class accommodation for visitors to Boscombe and could rival the large Bournemouth hotels.

Royal Arcade, Boscombe. When it opened in 1893, this stylish arcade was known as the Grand Continental Arcade. As part of a complex which included the Salisbury Hotel and the Grand Pavilion Theatre, the grandeur of the building ensured that Boscombe was seen as a fashionable and desirable neighbour to Bournemouth.

Boscombe Sands. This view hints at the popularity Boscombe had achieved by the turn of the century, especially once refreshment rooms, the pier and walks across the cliff had opened. Further to the east, Southbourne had developed its own features and was also attracting a good number of visitors.

Boscombe Pier, 1930s. By this time the pier has a more elaborate entrance and the Undercliff has its paved drive and promenade. It is interesting to compare this view with the first of this chapter. Within approximately seventy years it is apparent that although the area has gained the expected features of a seaside resort the underlying landscape is unchanged.

Steamship at Boscombe Pier. As with Bournemouth, the pier at Boscombe also acted as a landing stage for pleasure steamers.

Wharncliff Mansions, Christchurch Road. Gradually the road leading from Bournemouth to Boscombe was lined with housing and hotels, many of impressive architectural style and equally grand names.

CHAPTER ELEVEN
THE RUSSELL-COTES FAMILY

The life in Bournemouth of Merton and Annie Russell-Cotes provides an interesting example of the type of people who settled in the town, at what must have been an exciting and dynamic time for those with influence.

They first came to Bournemouth, from Glasgow, because of Merton's poor health and stayed at the Bath Hotel. The sea air lived up to its reputation and the couple liked and were impressed by the town. They decided to stay, and in 1876 the ambitious Merton bought the Bath Hotel; he spent four years making extensions and improvements. It reopened in 1880 and was a success.

As an interested citizen, Merton Russell-Cotes also became involved in local politics and the development of the town. He was involved in some major decisions, and sometimes his business interests may have had an influence in his continued perseverance to realise certain schemes. Merton became Mayor of Bournemouth in 1894.

Both Merton and Annie were keen collectors of fine and decorative arts and used the hotel to display treasures from their various trips abroad. In 1898 work was started on East Cliff Hall, a stunning house designed to be lived in by the family and for the further display of their collections. The architect was John Frederick Fogerty, and the house still draws attention on top of the East Cliff.

In 1908 the house and its contents were given to the town of Bournemouth and became the Russell-Cotes Art Gallery and Museum. For a town with little evident history compared with its older neighbours, the Russell-Cotes ensured that it would none the less have a museum of significant note.

Annie and Merton Russell-Cotes on their wedding day, February 1860. The couple had met six years previously, in 1854, and moved to Dublin after the marriage. They had five children in all, although two died in infancy.

East Cliff Hall, 1907. As much effort was put into the garden design as the house. It incorporated a grotto, Japanese garden, pergola, tropical plants, statues and urns to create a unique garden with a spectacular view out to sea.

The Gallery, 1907. Above the Hall, this upstairs balcony was used to display just some of the paintings in the house. It is interesting to see how they were displayed with barely a space between them.

The Hall, 1907.

The Drawing Room, 1907. The many treasures from different lands provided the greatest interest in the rooms of the house. Today, even the fixtures and fittings used provide a fascinating insight into the styles and extravagance of high Victorian society.

The Study, 1907. The interior of the house drew on various architectural styles, which were used to create a different setting and atmosphere in each room.

ACKNOWLEDGEMENTS

Many thanks are due to the Russell-Cotes Art Gallery and Museum for allowing me access to their photographic collection. Particular appreciation is due to Shaun Garner for his help in this respect.

I would also like to express gratitude to friends and family for their help and support.

Every effort has been made to trace all photograph copyright holders. If you have been omitted please contact the publisher, so that any future editions can be corrected. Historical information and identification of photographs is correct to the best of my knowledge, but alternative opinions will be respectfully received.

Other titles published by The History Press

A History of Bournemouth Seafront

ANDREW EMERY

Published to celebrate the renovation of Boscome pier, this is the definitive socal history of Bournemouth from the nineteeenth century when it was little more than a remote and barren heathland, its subsequent popularity as a spa resort in the Edwardian period, and its present status as a leading destination for family holidays.

978-0-7524-4717-9

Bournemouth Past

ELIZABETH EDWARDS

This book is an insight into the rich heritage of Bournemouth. It takes the reader on a journey through the places that made Bournemouth a popular destination for holidaymakers through the centuries and introduces the people, who helped create the town we know today.

978-0-8503-3962-8

Bournemouth's Airports: A History

MIKE PHIPPS

This is the history of Bournemouth Airport from its beginnings as RAF Hurn to its development as an international airport. The book charts the ups and downs of the airport, including sections on the First and Second World Wars, the local aviation industry, the gloom of the 1960s, new leadership, the National Express Group and the Manchester Airports Group. Mike Phipp finishes with a look to the future of Bournemouth International Airport and its capacity for handling 2 million passengers a year from 2009.

978-0-7524-3923-5

Weymouth & Portland

TED GOSLING

This superb collection of historic photographs takes the reader on a fascinating journey through the recent history of Weymouth and Portland. The book gives us unforgettable impression of familiar streets and districts as they developed, and offers an evocative insight into the daily lives of the local people and tourists in the last years of Queen Victoria's reign and the early years of this century.

978-0-7524-3066-9

Visit our website and discover thousands of other History Press books.

www.thehistorypress.co.uk